Between Weeks

To my wife, Silvia

Fred DeRuvo

Copyright © 2009 by Adroit Publications

All rights reserved. Written permission must be secured from the publisher to use or reproduce any part of this book, except brief quotations in critical reviews or articles.

Published in Scotts Valley, California, by Adroit Publications
www.adroitpublications.com • www.rightly-dividing.com

Scripture quotations are from The Holy Bible, English Standard Version®, copyright © 2001 by Crossway Bibles, a publishing ministry of Good News Publishers. Used by permission. All rights reserved.

Images used in this publication (unless otherwise noted) are from clipartconnection.com and used with permission, ©2007 JUPITERIMAGES, and its licensors. All rights reserved.

All Woodcuts used herein are in the Public Domain and free of copyright.

All Figure illustrations used in this book were created by the author and protected under copyright laws, © 2009.

Library of Congress Cataloging-in-Publication Data

DeRuvo, Fred, 1957 –

ISBN 1442189541
EAN-13 9781442189546

1. Religion – Biblical Studies – Exegesis and Hermeneutics

Foreword

I have wanted to write a book like this for a while. The subject has always interested me, primarily because while I see a clear break between the 69th and 70th week of Gabriel's prophecy to Daniel in chapter nine, I realize others do not. This is obviously not meant to be an exhaustive study, but an overview.

Prophecy has always intrigued me and it is not because I tend to think about the future and how God is and will work, although that helps. What intrigues me is realizing that God has stooped to reveal His plans to humanity. When the angel Gabriel arrived to relay to Daniel how the 70 weeks would unfold and what they ultimately meant for Israel and Jerusalem, he was essentially telling Daniel the future. The future he was learning about from Gabriel was the future that God Almighty had predetermined. There was no chance of it *not* happening the way it had been predetermined to occur. It was a future fact and the meaning of the 70 weeks would unfurl as God had foreordained.

We have at our disposal God's Word and the way it is interpreted will mean the difference between getting it right and getting it wrong. It is easy to become self-confident about what we believe God's Word says. If we are not careful, not long after self-confidence comes arrogance.

We need to clearly establish in our minds that we are reading the very words that God has chosen to share with us. Since that is the case, *everything* we read needs to be understood from *God's perspective*. That should be our goal.

I pray that as you read through this little book, you will benefit from it. I pray that the fire of desire will be lit within you; a desire to *know* Him through His Word, not only in the areas of prophetic discourse, but in all areas as He has revealed Himself to us.

May the Lord be glorified with my efforts and yours as well.

- Fred DeRuvo May 2009

Contents

Chapter 1:	The Answer Arrives	7
Chapter 2:	A Week is Not a Week	15
Chapter 3:	A Triplet of Weeks	24
Chapter 4:	In Between Races	38
Chapter 5:	Last Play of the Game	46
Chapter 6:	Seeing Things Clearly	56
Chapter 7:	A Race Well Run	64

ILLUSTRATIONS:

Figure 1: God Will Accomplish Six Things	23
Figure 2: Daniel 9: The 70 Weeks Chart	27
Figure 3: Overview of the Weeks Laid Out	29
Figure 4: Weeks in Detail	35

The List of Resources 69

Chapter 1

The Answer Arrives

Daniel is an extremely interesting book for any number of reasons. It provides a schematic of prophecy as it unfolds through the ages beginning with the Babylonian Empire, ruled by Nebuchadnezzar. The various chapters of Daniel reveal the different empires from Babylon to Medo-Persia, to Hellenistic to Roman and the ultimate empire headed by the Antichrist himself. The Antichrist stage will be a worldwide form of Absolute

Imperialism, in which the one man – Antichrist – has his way for three and a half years. He also gets his chance to marshal the world's troops in his own efforts to overthrow Christ and His coming reign. During the time the Antichrist is moving up the ranks to his final climactic grab for power, it will literally become hell on earth. This is no mere metaphor. Numerous places in Daniel, Revelation, Ezekiel, Joel and elsewhere refer to other worldly beings literally coming forth from the *pit* to inflict pain, damage or death on the inhabitants of this world and the physical earth itself.

By the time we get to the ninth chapter of Daniel, we find that Daniel has been studying the writings of the prophet Jeremiah. This has brought him to the understanding that the 70 years of captivity of Israel's southern kingdom under the Babylonians is almost at an end.

The resultant encouragement Daniel felt from reading Jeremiah translated into the realization that the time of freedom appeared to be near at hand. Because of this, Daniel turns his attention to the Lord, entering into an intense time of prayer. He confesses Israel's sin and his sin, acting as priest for the nation. He then beseeches the Lord to reveal to him exactly when the time will come that Israel will once again be free of her captors.

It Was Literal
It is interesting to note here that Daniel had no difficulty taking the predictions in Jeremiah of seventy years in a *literal* fashion (cf. Jeremiah 25:11-12). To Daniel, Jeremiah said seventy years and seventy years is what he meant. There could be no other meaning. Certainly Daniel was not an idiot. He understood that at times God used highly symbolic imagery to express aspects of His prophetic will. Even there though, he understood those symbols to have specific meanings associated with them. Daniel seemed able to understand when something was meant to be understood from a symbolic point of view and from a literal.

It is because of this understanding, Daniel goes to the Lord in prayer, realizing that because God is sovereign, His will is predetermined. Yet at the same time, there is the responsibility on man to invest himself in God's purposes as they are revealed to us. Daniel was a man who knew the importance of prayer, praying three times daily with his window open toward Jerusalem. It is not surprising then that with the revelation of this new information regarding the fact that the seventy years had nearly expired, Daniel entered into reverent and humble prayer with the Lord God of Israel.

A Prayer of Prayers
It is fascinating that as Daniel prayed, he confirmed God's faithfulness to His covenants, in spite of the fact that Israel constantly and consistently rebelled against God. He marveled and extolled God's grace, His righteousness, His love and His faithfulness. He admitted Israel's lack of all of these toward God and their unwillingness to bend their knee to God Almighty. Daniel did this for the nation, as he prayed a high priestly prayer on behalf of his people, fellow Jews, the Israelites. He certainly expected no special favors at all, but hoped for them. He condemned Israel's pride and arrogance and her inability to remain faithful. He admitted that Israel got what she deserved because of the iniquity in which they wallowed.

It is also enthralling that Daniel is one of the well known individuals of the Bible of whom it can be said was essentially without sin. What I mean here is not that he was perfect because he was not. What I mean is that there is no record of him succumbing to some *major* sin as did David, Samson, and many others whose lives are an open book in Scripture for us today. Daniel had a sin nature as we all do, and it is certainly accurate to say he gave into it at times throughout his life. However, there is nothing that we can point to which would show a time where he fell and fell mightily because of sin. Such is not the case.

Daniel's prayer requesting forgiveness is prayed on behalf of the nation of Israel. He recognizes and admits her sin, confessing it before the God who sees all, asking that His forgiveness would extend to Israel. The humility evidenced in Daniel's prayer and in the man himself is palpable. Israel had become an embarrassment for other nations by profaning the name of God. These nations saw her disobedience and the many temporary rejections of her by God. It appeared God was actually working *against* Israel by not protecting her from invasion. What these nations did not realize of course is that God was using them as His arm of judgment to chastise Israel. He would then turn His judgment on these same invading entities who dared to touch the Apple of God's eye!

While Daniel is still in prayer, the answer comes to him in the form of the "man" Gabriel. It is noteworthy what Gabriel tells Daniel here, even before he provides the answer regarding the 70 year captivity; *"O Daniel, I have now come out to give you insight and understanding. At the beginning of your pleas for mercy a word went out, and I have come to tell it to you, for you are greatly loved. Therefore consider the word and understand the vision,"* (Dan 9:22b-23). What a wonderful thing to hear! Is there anything more blessed that could be said of anyone? Daniel was "greatly loved" by God and it was due to Daniel's faithfulness that the Lord loved him as he did. Daniel was a humble man, continually seeking the Lord's will in all things. He is an example for all of us who strive to be like Christ.

After this greeting, Gabriel goes on to relate to Daniel the details of the prophecy, beginning in verse 24 through 27. These four verses are likely four of the most important verses in all of Scripture. The reality is that Satan is completely aware of their importance as well and has done (and continues to do) whatever he can to muddy their message, burying the truth under layers of error and deception. Because of that, we have the error of Replacement Theology, which teaches that Israel was superseded by the Church; completely replaced. Therefore, according to this view, Israel is no more. She is gone forever, replaced by the Church.

However, in these four verses, we see a completely different picture, which includes the infamous *parenthesis* that is said to exist between the 69th and 70th weeks. It is this parenthesis that indicates which part of the 70 weeks we are living in today. We will go through this step by step, and the reader will hopefully see and understand that not only is the parenthesis *not* man-made, but is absolutely included in God's Word.

For now, please note that Gabriel has been sent by the Lord to explain to Daniel the meaning of the 70 years of captivity and the length of time that exists for it.

This is why Gabriel arrived. He is described by Daniel as a "man" in verse 21, because to Daniel this is how he looked. It is clear though that this "man" is certainly supernatural in origin because of the complete description given, "*while I was speaking in prayer, the man Gabriel, whom I had seen in the vision at the first, came to me in swift flight at the time of the evening sacrifice,*" (Dan 9:21). The phrase "swift flight" signifies an angelic being, not merely a man. So we can take from this that while Gabriel *looked* like a man, he was anything *but* a man. Of course, having been sent by God confirms this.

It appears that God wanted to assure Daniel that His purposes still stood. He was still on the throne and His sovereignty was not in question. His purposes for Israel would yet be fulfilled, as He had first promised to Abraham in Genesis 12:1-3.

Gabriel was sent by God to fill in the blanks so to speak with respect to Israel's future. It is this that leads into his unveiling of the Seventy Sevens of Weeks, which only appear in this section of the entire Bible.

Starting in verse 24, Gabriel explains the interpretation of the passage that caused Daniel to ask his question, Jeremiah 25:12. This passage states *"Then after seventy years are completed, I will punish the king of Babylon and that nation, the land of the Chaldeans, for their iniquity, declares the Lord, making the land an everlasting waste,"* (Jeremiah 25:12). Reference is also made in Ezra 1:1 regarding the decree to build a house for God in Jerusalem. Unfortunately, things do not really get going until Nehemiah, when he is given permission *and* commission to actually rebuild Jerusalem and the wall which at one point stood around it.

The End is Near?
Because of Daniel's zeal for the Lord and desire to see the Lord's will accomplished, he had been busy reading Jeremiah, meditating on the words of that prophet. This led him to conclude that since the 70 years of captivity spoken about by Jeremiah were almost up, which then caused him to seek the Lord in prayer.

The prayer of Daniel is one of the great priestly prayers of God's Word. In it, Daniel intercedes for his people, Israel, admitting their gross failure to believe God, constantly testing His patience and love. On behalf of Israel, he confesses their national sin. The entirety of the prayer is found in verses eight through nineteen of chapter nine. I would encourage the reader to pause and read through that prayer a number of times before moving on.

One of things that becomes quickly evident here is that Daniel pulls no punches regarding the people of Israel. He makes no excuses for them, admitting their guilt before God. In verse eleven, he makes the statement *"All Israel has transgressed your law and turned aside, refusing to obey your voice,"* (Dan 9:11). It is not at all difficult to see why Daniel was loved as he was, because he laid his soul bare before the Lord on this and all occasions in his life. He did not seek to provide Israel with any type of excuse for their behavior, but readily admitted that what they did was sin. He called it sin, something that many have an aversion to in today's world. We shy away from using the word "sin" because it sounds way too *judgmental*. This is in spite of the fact that Jesus spoke more about hell than any other topic.

The problem though is that the word "sin" *should* be used and used on a regular basis to describe those times we fail to obey the Lord. However, as I have written in another work, God does *not* want us to beat ourselves up over are sin. What He wants us to do is provide *no* excuse for our sin, but to confess it to Him, with contrition. We then need to move onto the cross, reminding ourselves that this sin, as all of our sin, was dealt with at Calvary's cross and it is gone. Our prayer of confession should end in praise for His glorious and victorious work on Golgotha's hill, where His precious blood was shed in order that we might be cleansed with it and have life eternal. Praise His Name for His mighty provision, which includes His forgiveness.

Had Daniel finished his prayer, he would likely have ended with praise. He started by confessing Israel's sin, offering no excuses for it, and accepting their current fate as God's judgment on their sin. He had gotten to the point in his prayer of beginning to ask the Lord to visit Israel once again; "*Now therefore, O our God, listen to the prayer of your servant and to his pleas for mercy, and for your own sake, O Lord, make your face to shine upon your sanctuary, which is desolate. O my God, incline your ear and hear. Open your eyes and see our desolations, and the city that is called by your name. For we do not present our pleas before you because of our righteousness, but because of your great mercy. O Lord, hear; O Lord, forgive. O Lord, pay attention and act. Delay not, for your own sake, O my God, because your city and your people are called by your name,*" (Dan 9:17-19).

It was at this point he was interrupted, unable to finish. Daniel was so loved that he did not even *need* to finish his prayer before the answer came in this case. Gabriel tells him this as we read in verse twenty-three "*At the beginning of your pleas for mercy a word went out, and I have come to tell it to you,*" (Dan 9:23). Would that our prayers were heard as quickly by God. The key is in praying for His will in all things; not our will. While it is fine to ask, there must always be room left for God to do what His will specifies, which may or may not be what we are praying for at that moment. This is made significantly clear to us in the Garden of Gethsemane, when Christ prayed that the situation ahead of Him would be removed, but He was careful to add *"nevertheless, not my will but yours be done,"* (Luke 22:42).

Studying to Show Himself Worthy
So we see that this is the situation that exists for Daniel. He seemed to always be studying the Word; in this case Jeremiah. He seemed to always want to learn the Lord's will and to accomplish it. This was his life and his attitude. It was because of this life and attitude that he was blessed with direct answers to prayer which shed light on prophetic passages of Scripture.

As indicated, this particular passage of Scripture is one which provides unyielding light on the future coming of the Messiah and beyond to His Second Coming. Is it any wonder that Satan has attempted to mire this passage in total confusion?

Chapter 2

When A Week is Not a Week

The passage in Daniel 9 opens blind eyes, or at least is meant to, and in Daniel's case, it does. What I mean by that is simply that Daniel *thought* he knew the answer, but did not until Gabriel clarified for him. It was because of his humility before the Lord though that he was provided the answer. That answer blesses us today, *if* we will receive it how it is *meant*.

Replacement Theology as well as Covenant Theology and Preterism all claim that Israel has been *replaced* by the Church. Therefore, because of this, Israel is no more. She is gone; she's history; kaput. Because Israel rejected her Messiah, crucifying Him, God's patience had run out (their view) and it was due to this, that He utterly and permanently broke fellowship with Israel, completely and totally casting them aside. In this author's opinion, the eyes of the individuals who believe this remain closed to the truth. They seem unable or unwilling (maybe both), to *hear* what Gabriel has clearly stated.

An Unbiblical Position
This is an unfortunate position to accept as true and espouse, because it is completely *unbiblical*. People hear and read this phrase a great deal from theologians on both sides of many issues. However, there is really nothing in Scripture (*if* Scripture is allowed to speak for itself), that lends support to this errant view of God's dealings with either the Church or Israel.

If we consider all of the times that Israel completely and utterly failed God by refusing to believe Him, which led to rebellion and disobedience, we never see a time when God cast Israel away from Himself *permanently*. He always emphasized His faithfulness in spite of Israel's disobedience. Yet, we are to now believe that God finally came to a point of realizing that His continuing with Israel was hopeless. Left with nothing else, He abandoned them, creating a new entity instead from which there would be no difference between the Jew or Gentile, man or woman, free or slave. Unfortunately, it appears that this view makes God the one who reneges on His promises. In this case, the promises were stated to Abraham not once, but on at least three separate occasions in the book of Genesis alone, and then to others who came after Abraham as well.

Yet, the theologians who believe that God *did* toss Israel aside do so based solely on Israel's rejection of Jesus as Messiah. It is clear from the Old Testament alone that the Messiah was to be rejected and would die as a direct result of that rejection. Since God saw, knew and even designed this to occur, it is difficult to believe that this rejection was God's "final straw." This is especially difficult to grasp considering the specific promises to Abraham that He made. While the Gentiles would benefit (all the families of the earth will be blessed through Abraham; Genesis 12:1-3), they would benefit from the availability of *salvation*. The other promises made to Abraham were specifically made for the future nation of Israel.

God's Rejection Has Never Been Permanent
We will see that Daniel 9 clearly indicates that the Messiah was to be killed, long before it happened. We will also note that every time Israel rejected God in some form, judgment always came. This was the reason that Israel (the southern kingdom) was now in captivity to Babylon. They had once again rejected God, refusing to comply with His rule over them.

Every time Israel rejects God, He sends judgment on them. This is usually through a neighboring empire, who sweeps in, destroys much of their population, then takes the remaining Israelites alive as slaves. This happened time and time again. They are usually tossed or carried out of their own land, which normally includes Jerusalem. They are then dispersed into the world among their captives.

Eventually though, God always brings them back to their own land where they once again enjoy the city of Jerusalem, God's center of the world, and peace with Him. There is no reason to believe that God always intended at one point to drop Israel like a hot potato permanently. The Scriptures indicate otherwise.

Israel's path has always been a series of obeying God, then rejecting Him. They are then restored to fellowship after a time of misery, leading to repentance. They begin to cry out to God (usually a new generation of Jews), and God turns His ear to them. He then brings them out of captivity back to their homeland. That is the cycle and in essence, they are in the very end of that "dispersion" part of that cycle now. We can see since 1948, that they have begun making their way back to Israel. However, in this current case, it is noteworthy to understand that though this author believes God is in charge of bringing them back to the land, the Israelites themselves are unaware of it. They have not called out to Him. They are merely being brought back to the land. It is because of what God said through Ezekiel chapters 20, 22, 37 and other passages of Scripture as well. God will gather Israel together again into His land and He will do it while they are still in *unbelief*. This certainly describes Israel today and since 1948 when they once again became a sovereign state, recognized by the U.N.

The 70 Weeks of Daniel
Getting back to Daniel and the answer to his prayer, Gabriel begins to instruct Daniel regarding the 70 years of captivity. He explains what is going to happen to Israel in verse twenty-four, *"Seventy weeks are decreed about your people and your holy city, to finish the transgression, to put an end to sin, and to atone for iniquity, to bring in everlasting righteousness, to seal both vision and prophet, and to anoint a most holy place. Know therefore and understand that from the going out of the word to restore and build Jerusalem to the coming of an anointed one, a prince, there shall be seven weeks. Then for sixty-two weeks it shall be built again with squares and moat, but in a troubled time. And after the sixty-two weeks, an anointed one shall be cut off and shall have nothing. And the people of the prince who is to come shall destroy the city and the sanctuary. Its end shall come with a flood, and to the end there shall be war. Desolations are decreed. And he shall make a strong covenant with many for one week, and for half of the week he shall put an end to sacrifice and offering. And on the wing of abominations shall come one who makes desolate, until the decreed end is poured out on the desolator,"* (Dan 9:24-27).

The People and the Holy City
It is extremely important to understand exactly *who* Gabriel is referencing here. He starts off by saying that *"Seventy weeks are decreed*

*about **your people** and **your holy city**...*" (emphasis added) Right away we understand that Gabriel is referring to *Daniel's* people (Israel, the Jews) and *Daniel's* holy city (Jerusalem), and he is clearly indicating that this is a *sovereign* plan by God Almighty, hence the use of the word *decreed* (or *determined*). God made the plan and will carry it out to its fulfillment. We can assume that it *will* come to full fruition and it *will* bring glory to Him as well. This is *the* reason God does anything.

There is no other way to interpret the text. It is clear that Gabriel is referring to Israel and Jerusalem. It can be taken no other way, unless the passage is allegorized, in which case another meaning can be superimposed over the text to refer to the Church. But this is obviously not the case if we leave the text alone as it is, and understand it in its most normal, logical sense.

In this case, there is absolutely *no* reason to allegorize Scripture at this point. There is nothing that indicates it *should* be allegorized. To do so then, is to do damage to the text, by changing God's intended meaning.

Gabriel is telling Daniel that seventy *weeks* are determined. Someone might come along and say "Hey, the word *weeks*; what about that? Shouldn't that be taken literally as well?" Yes, it should absolutely be taken literally; no question. Let's take a close look at the word "weeks" then to see what we can learn about it.

Doing a brief word study on this word provides the following information. We note that the Hebrew word here is *shābûá*. This particular Hebrew word literally means "*a period of sevens.*"[1]

Seventy What?
The text then should actually read like this "Seventy *sevens* are decreed about your people..." But what does that tell us; seventy se-

---

[1] Stephen D. Renn, Ed., *Expository Dictionary of Bible Words* (Peabody: Hendriksen 2005),1036

vens of *what*? Gabriel's use of the word *sevens* here is as Dr. Arnold G. Fruchtenbaum says a bit of a play on words (cf. Footsteps of the Messiah). What Gabriel is saying in essence is "Daniel, it's not 70 weeks, but 70 sevens of weeks."

In other words, the term *sevens* here is no different than when we might say in English that we were going to buy a *dozen* eggs. The word dozen in itself does *not* say what the dozen refers to, but merely indicates a *quantity*. It could be a dozen *eggs*, a dozen, *golf balls*, a dozen *gallons of milk*, a dozen *cupcakes*, or anything else where a dozen might be used. We know of course that the word *dozen* equals twelve. However, that number only specifies quantity, not the article itself, which is why it can be used with any number of specific items.

In this way Gabriel is saying to Daniel that 70 sevens are determined for the Jews. So how do we know what the *sevens* actually refers to here? Gabriel does *not* follow it up with a specific word like *days* for instance. The meaning of *sevens* is found in the *context* of the entire chapter.

We know from the second verse of chapter nine that Daniel had been dealing with *years*, "*I, Daniel, perceived in the books the number of* **years** *that, according to the word of the Lord to Jeremiah the prophet, must pass before the end of the desolations of Jerusalem, namely,* **seventy years**," (Dan 9:2; emphasis added).

490 Years Total
It is here that we learn Daniel was thinking in terms of *years*. That is clear from the text and indisputable. When Gabriel arrives, he clarifies for Daniel that it is not seventy *years,* but in reality it will wind up being *seventy sevens of years.* Seventy sevens of years equal a total of 490 years (70 x 7). This is where we get the 490 years. So far, so good. We have not pointed out the parenthesis yet, but we will get to that. We have merely provided the total number of prophetic years

in which God has decreed for Israel and the Holy City. This then is God's timeframe; 490 years.

Notice that Gabriel explains to Daniel *why* 490 years has been established for Israel. He points to six things we see in the text (vv. 24-25; see **Figure 1**):

1. To finish the transgression
2. To put an end to sin
3. To atone for the iniquity
4. To bring in everlasting righteousness
5. To seal both vision and prophet
6. To anoint a most holy place

These six things are what God planned to occur as the *reason* for the 490 years, related to the people of Israel and the Holy City. At the end of it, all six of those things will have occurred and God will be glorified.

Looking at that list, it is easy to see that this is *not* the case now with Israel, as a nation. She continues in unbelief, which of course is sin. Certainly no one would argue that Israel *presently* exists in a state of everlasting righteousness.

Maybe In the Spiritual Realm?
But this is also where some theologians transfer all of this to the Church declaring that in the *spiritual realm*, these things *do* exist. However, the only way they can get to that interpretation is by allegorizing the text. Yet, it is very clear from the passage itself that Gabriel is not allegorizing anything, therefore neither should we.

We must consider just how much information God provided to Abraham, or to many of the other prophets, yet never told any of them that He had plans to create a unique entity of believers which was going to be called the Church. It becomes extremely difficult then to simply take any remaining promises that are directed to Israel and transfer them to the Church.

Was the Church Really Kept a Secret?
The fact that God indicated beginning with Abraham that through him, all nations would be blessed, tells us that God had *always* intended to extend the gospel to the Gentiles. There is certainly no argument there. Every prophet of the Old Testament understood that. What they did *not* understand was the fact that God would set aside Israel *temporarily* (but not *permanently*), in order to create this unique body of believers – the Church – which would then be the vehicle He would use to introduce the gospel to all nations apart from Israel.

There is no need to *transfer* anything from Israel to the Church, especially since we know that the gospel message carries with it only *one* method of salvation. This has *always* been the case, unless you are a Covenant Theologian. The Covenant Theologian believes that at one point in time, salvation was *earned* by works. This is why they call the time period with Adam the "Covenant of Works" because they declare that Adam was specifically under a banner of works-related effort in order to obtain salvation. This is not the case though as this author has shown in another work titled *Dispensationalism's View of God's Sovereignty*. Salvation has *always* been and *continues* to be by grace, through faith, in Christ. There is nothing added to it, in spite of the detrimental teaching of Covenant Theology.

Summing Up Before Moving Ahead
We know that Gabriel is stating to Daniel that seventy sevens of weeks is decreed for Israel and the Holy City of Jerusalem. We also know that the word *weeks* here means *years*. In the end then, we know that Gabriel is literally stating that 490 years are decreed in full for Israel. Now we can move on to the next part of Gabriel's explanation.

FIGURE 1 - God Will Accomplish Six Things with Israel

Finish the Transgression

Israel's rebellion needs to come to an end.

God will do that before the 2nd Coming of Christ

To Make an End to Sin

Unlike Christ, Israel committed sins daily, which stem from their rebellious attitude

To Make Atonement for Iniquity

While Jesus atoned for Israel's sins, it will not be applied until Israel accepts Him as Messiah (this refers to the NATION of Israel, not individual Jews)

To Bring in Everlasting Righteousness

When Israel repents and believes in Christ as Messiah at His 2nd Coming, she will be given lasting righteousness at that point.

To Seal Up the Vision & Prophecy

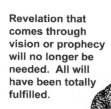

Revelation that comes through vision or prophecy will no longer be needed. All will have been totally fulfilled.

To Anoint the Most Holy Place

Consecrating the articles of the Temple or Tabernacle

Chapter 3

A Triplet of Weeks

U nderstanding the length of time that Gabriel is referring to is necessary in order to understand the entire explanation and subsequent scenario. By arriving at the correct conclusion here, the rest of the text nearly falls into place by itself.

The Starting Point
There is one other place in Gabriel's explanation which needs particular care. If not understood properly, the entire scope of the *paren-*

thesis will be completely missed. Let's take another look at the text, beginning with verse twenty-five.

"Know therefore and understand that from the going out of the word to restore and build Jerusalem to the coming of an anointed one, a prince, there shall be seven weeks, then for sixty-two weeks it shall be built again with squares and moat, but in a troubled time," (Dan 9:25). Gabriel states that from the going out of the word to restore and build Jerusalem, etc., there will be *seven sevens* (weeks) plus the *sixty-two sevens*, for a total of *69 weeks*.

We need to determine two things; 1) what "word" to restore Jerusalem is Gabriel referring to here and 2) how long is seven sevens?

Different starting dates have been put forth based on a number of decrees issued by individual rulers to rebuild Jerusalem. For instance, one such decree was issued by Cyrus and we find reference to this in Ezra 4:12-21, when the walls surrounding Jerusalem were to be rebuilt. However, there is no evidence within Ezra that the walls *were* either started or finished in 457 B.C.

The difficulty here is that according to Nehemiah, who came after Ezra, it is clear that the walls were in complete disrepair. The city itself was in such bad shape that Nehemiah could not travel through with the beast he came with (cf. Nehemiah 2). At this point also, it is very clear that though many Jews had already *returned* to the *area* of Jerusalem, all of them were living *outside* the city in homes, yet the Temple of the Lord was in shambles. In Nehemiah 11, they actually had to draw lots to see who would go back into Jerusalem proper to live there, because no one wanted to do so!

It seems apparent enough from all the historical data and internal evidence of Scripture that the most obvious choice of starting point is with Artaxerxes Longimanus. He ruled Persia from 465 – 425 B.C. and he is also the one who had commissioned Ezra to go back to Jerusalem in 457 B.C. Even though other decrees were given to various individuals to rebuild, it was not until Longimanus gave the order to *Nehemiah* to rebuild Jerusalem in 445 B.C. that the building actually began. Most scholars indicate the exact day is equivalent to March 14, 445 B.C. on our calendar.

Nehemiah's Starting Point
The opening verses of Nehemiah 2 present us with the information needed; that this particular decree went forth from Artaxerxes in the twentieth year of his reign. Because Nehemiah is so clear regarding this, most scholars have agreed that the decree Gabriel is referring to came from Artaxerxes Longimanus in 445 B.C.

It *must* be remembered that Gabriel is speaking to Daniel about *Israel* and about *Jerusalem*. This means that any dates he implicates to Daniel would be on the *God's prophetic* calendar, which is based not only 365 days, but *360* days per year. We need to keep that in mind as we move through this text.

Gabriel tells Daniel that from that particular starting point to the coming of the anointed One and the rebuilding of Jerusalem (whom Gabriel refers to as *the prince*), there will be a total of sixty-nine sevens, or 483 years (69 years times 7). If 445 B.C. is our starting point, then it is merely the matter of moving 483 years into the future (from Daniel's perspective) to see where we end up.

If we move ahead from 445 B.C., 483 years later, we find ourselves right at the Triumphal Entry of Christ into Jerusalem.

We can see the information charted out that has just been provided in **Figure 2**. From March 14, 445 B.C. to the Triumphal Entry, which occurred on April 6, 32 A.D., a total of 173,880 *days* passed (again, based on the Jewish calendar of 360 days per year). This is the same as 483 years, or 69 weeks.

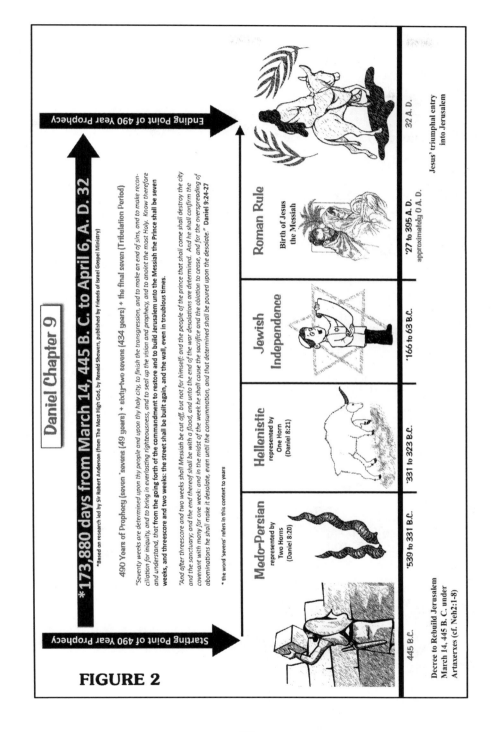

FIGURE 2

The 69 weeks make up the first *two* periods of time; 7 weeks (49 years) and 62 weeks (434 years; 49 + 434 = 483 years).

The Parenthesis

All right, *now let's* discuss the parenthesis. Almost everyone has heard about the infamous *parenthesis* or *gap* in the time period here being relayed by Gabriel. Many say they do not see it; can't find it; it's not there; somebody's making it up, etc.

The truth of the matter is that it *is* there and it is *unmistakably* delineated in the text itself. I wonder if people are looking too hard for it and in doing so, have missed it completely? If the text is merely read as it is, it is difficult *not* to see it. The trouble usually arises from coming to the text with preconceived suppositions regarding its meaning. In this case, whether we like it or not, or are willing to admit to it, we are reading into the text. Because of that, certain things will remain hidden to us because we do not want to see them, as they do not fall in line with what we already believe about the text.

The cover of this book highlights the four verses of Daniel 9 and their implications. That same illustration is also included within these pages so that it can all be clearly seen and how each verse relates its detail. See **Figure 4**, page 35.

We have looked at the text up to the end of verse twenty-five, which as shown provides us with the 483 year period of time. This was to have run consecutively and *then* we see a break, or parenthesis.

Returning to the text, we read these words *"And after the sixty-two weeks, an anointed one shall be cut off and shall have nothing. And the people of the prince who is to come shall destroy the city and the sanctuary. Its end shall come with a flood, and to the end there shall be war. Desolations are decreed,"* (Dan 9:26).

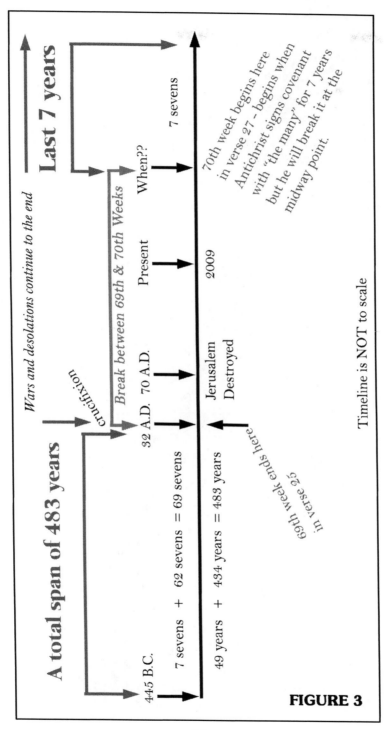
FIGURE 3

The first few words provide the key to the parenthesis and we have provided another chart in **Figure 3** which highlights this information. The text says *"And after the sixty-two weeks..."* From this, we can see that while there was no break or parenthesis *before,* during the two previous time periods of 7 weeks and 62 weeks (49 years + 434 years), there *is* a parenthesis here because Gabriel is essentially saying, *"Daniel the first 7 weeks and 62 weeks taken together bring us up to the coming of the Anointed One. It is after these two time periods that three things occur."* That is *literally* what Gabriel is saying. That signifies the parenthesis, or gap. All we need to do is understand what is coming *after* the 7 weeks and 62 weeks. Fortunately, we do not have to guess at all, because Gabriel tells Daniel (and us):

1. An Anointed One shall be cut off and will have nothing
2. The people of the prince to come will destroy the city and the sanctuary, with a flood
3. To the end there shall be war and desolations are determined

It is clear then that these three things *must* occur immediately *after* the 69 weeks (483 years), and *before* the 70th week (which is detailed in the next verse, verse twenty-seven. So Gabriel is stating that *before* the details of verse twenty-seven can occur, the three things he lists in verse twenty-six *must* take place.

Walvoord points out that *"practically all expositors agree that the death of Christ occurred after the sixty-ninth seven."*[2]

It's All About Jesus

Though some expositors disagree with this, the majority say the text appears to be a clear reference to Jesus as the Messiah. If this is so, then it can be proven that Jesus was the Messiah from this book and chapter alone. No Christian should be without this information because you never *know* when God will have you in a perfect position to

---

[2] John F. Walvoord *Daniel the Key to Prophetic Revelation* (Chicago: Moody Press 1971), 228

witness to an individual of Jewish background, or Gentile for that matter.

In spite of what appears to be a clear reference to Christ, some view the individual in question as simply being a secular ruler whom God chooses to use, as in Cyrus, who issued a decree, or Artaxerxes who issued another decree. Walvoord tells us that *"By far, the majority of scholars who accept Daniel as a genuine book find the reference in verse 25 to Jesus Christ."*[3]

The entire passage must be taken as a whole. Gabriel is stating that "an anointed one" will be "cut off." We know that Jesus was certainly anointed of the Father, which occurred during his public baptism. We also know that if the 445 B.C. is the correct date for the decree that was issued to rebuild Jerusalem, then the 69 sevens of weeks would take us to the time of Christ's Triumphal Entry into Jerusalem. So while we need to understand the words used here, it is equally important to understand them in light of the passage's context.

The other important point to consider is just how important Jesus is in the overall prophetic discourse evidenced throughout the entirety of the Old Testament. It becomes doubtful that this particular passage, which appears to be so important for Israel, would be pointing merely to some *secular* ruler in their history, while most prophecy in the Old Testament somehow ties to Christ directly.

Walvoord again, *"The prominence of the Messiah in the Old Testament prophecy and the mention of Him in both verses 25 and 26 make the cutting off of the Messiah one of the important events in the prophetic unfoldment of God's plan for Israel and the world. How tragic that, when the promised King came, He was 'cut off.'"*[4]

---

[3] John F. Walvoord *Daniel the Key to Prophetic Revelation* (Chicago: Moody Press 1971), 229
[4] Ibid, 229

In Christ we see not only someone who was brutally and painfully executed, but we see Someone who died and who literally had *nothing*. The disciples had fled for fear of their own persecution and on the cross, Jesus Himself cried out asking why God had *forsaken* Him. He was truly alone; cut off from every other individual in the entire universe as His life bled away.

Cut Off

So it would appear that the text is indicating that the Anointed One shall be *cut off*. This means that the Anointed One will *come to an end, or* be *killed*. After the 483 years, the Messiah finally appears. Jesus at that time heralded His kingship as He rode into Jerusalem on a donkey. It is noteworthy to realize that the people were singing praise to Him in the form of Psalm 118. According to Dr. Chuck Missler, this Psalm "is a Hallel Psalm proclaiming Him as the Messiah: 'Blessed be the King that cometh in the name of the Lord: peace in heaven, and glory in the highest.'"[5]

Of particular interest here is the fact that Jesus fulfilled Zechariah 9:9, which reads *"Rejoice greatly, O daughter of Zion! Shout aloud, O daughter of Jerusalem! Behold, your king is coming to you; righteous and having salvation is he, humble and mounted on a donkey, on a colt, the foal of a donkey,"* (Zechariah 9:9).

The above verse is an obvious reference to the First Coming of the Messiah. Also interesting is the next verse, which reads *"I will cut off the chariot from Ephraim and the war horse from Jerusalem; and the battle bow shall be cut off, and he shall speak peace to the nations; his rule shall be from sea to sea, and from the River to the ends of the earth,"* (Zechariah 9:10). This verse is a reference to Christ's Second Coming, and please notice the Bible gives no indication that any time has passed at all. This occurs many times in Scripture and the only

---

[5] Dr. Chuck Missler, *Learn the Bible in 24 Hours*, (Nashville: Nelson Publishing 2002), 109

way to determine that there is a gap of time there is by comparing Scripture with Scripture!

We know that shortly after Jesus rode into Jerusalem and was pronounced King by the people, He was crucified. This is what Gabriel told Daniel would happen many years before it did.

This is the beauty of the Bible, as the many proofs found within prophecies point to the fact that God is who He says He is and He is Truth. He has graciously stooped to us, because of His infinite love for us. He has granted us knowledge that we had no right to know, yet He chose to reveal it to us, and most of us choose to misinterpret it.

Once Jesus rode into Jerusalem, the 69th week came to an end; however this is also up for debate, because not all see the events of verse 26 as occurring during an *interim*, but merely Gabriel providing more detail about the 69th week to the 70th, or the start of the 70th.

Yet, it is difficult to arrive at a conclusion other than the Messiah's death occurring *after* the 69th week because of what Gabriel told Daniel as recorded in verse 25. From the time the decree was *given*, until the *coming* of an anointed One, the Prince, was to be a total of 69 weeks. Jesus presented Himself as King as He rode into Jerusalem on that day just prior to His crucifixion.

The Things *After*
What Gabriel says next is extremely important. He continues by stating "And after this..." which should clearly be taken to mean *after* the 69th week, when the Anointed One arrived on the scene as King. It would appear that Gabriel is clearly stating that the coming of the anointed One, the Prince takes us to the end of the 69th week.

It is here that Gabriel states what is to take place *after* the 69th week, and we listed those already a few pages back. Now, once the Messiah was *cut off* or killed, the next event to take place is the destruction of

Jerusalem and the sanctuary (Temple). This is the very Temple that Jesus referred to at the beginning of His Olivet Discourse, found in Matthew, Mark and Luke. This particular Temple was a beautiful Temple built by Herod, who as it turns out according to the historical record, was a masterful designer.

We know that Jesus was crucified (and we also know He rose from the dead), and we know that the destruction of Jerusalem and the Temple occurred in A.D. 70. We also know who destroyed Jerusalem and the Temple. It was the Romans under Vespasian and Titus. This is historical fact which cannot be denied. These events are foretold by Gabriel in verse 26 of Daniel 9. The disagreement lies over exactly where they occur within the timeframe of God's prophetic calendar.

Verse 26 continues by stating "*And the people of the prince who is to come shall destroy the city and the sanctuary.*" We need only ask ourselves "*Who destroyed the city and the sanctuary?*" The correct answer is the *Romans*, as mentioned.

Gabriel ties the Romans with the *prince* in that verse "*and the people OF THE prince WHO IS TO COME shall destroy the city.*" The words "WHO IS TO COME" refer *directly* to the word *prince* here. This prince who is yet to come (implying that this prince has *not* come *yet*, so it cannot be Jesus), will be the prince of the *people who will destroy* the city and the sanctuary (yet future from Daniel's point of view). Since we know the Romans destroyed Jerusalem and the Temple, then this leader is obviously the *prince* of the *Roman* people. The point here is that the Romans and this *prince* are of the same nationality - *Gentile*.

God often used other armies or peoples or empires to judge Israel. While God *judged* Israel by destroying the city of Jerusalem and the Sanctuary, He has almost *always* used a people to perform His judgments. Normally then, those He uses as His arm of judgment are *also* later judged directly by God or through another group of people.

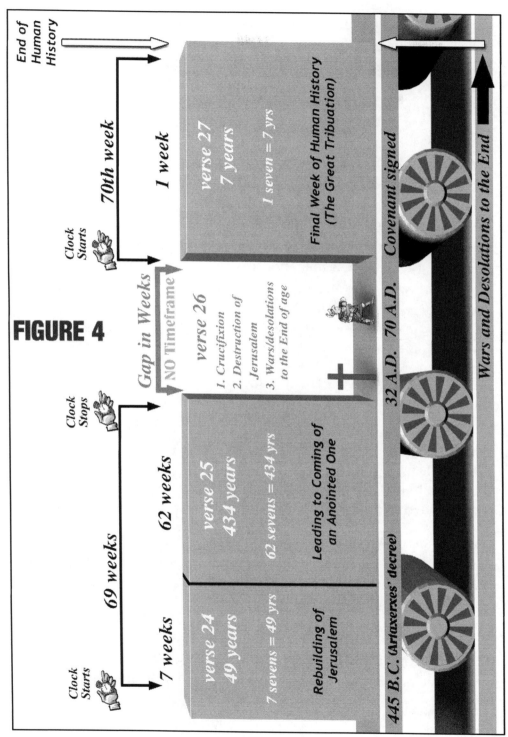

So, Gabriel is referring to a specific people - *the Romans*. Christ was *never* their prince. The Antichrist on the other hand, will be Gentile and of Roman descent, which may mean that he springs up in Europe, but who knows? In any case, the Antichrist will be of the same ethnicity as the Romans, which could mean merely Gentile, or Roman Gentile.

When the text says "*there will be wars and desolations to the end*" (my paraphrase), it means exactly that - there will be wars and desolations until the end. Is there a time in history *after* the Crucifixion when the entire world has been at peace? Moreover, is there a time in history when *Israel* has been in peace? She has not. To this *day*, she is at war with their neighboring nations. There are also plenty of rumors of war in the Middle East as well. Remember, the *entire* prophecy is directed to Daniel's *people* and Daniel's *holy city*. There is *no* reason to allegorize this and apply another meaning to it. Gabriel *means* Israelites and Jerusalem. It is clear and it is simple.

The 69th week actually comes to an end in verse 25, with verse 26 merely going on from that point. So the three events clearly occur *after* the 69th week, but *before* the 70th week. How do we know this? Because it is apparent from the text that the 70th week does not begin until one specific event takes place. That event is the covenant "he" makes with Israel for seven years. Seven years is the exact amount of time needed to complete the 70 weeks. It represents the last *seven*.

But how do we know that someone is going to make a covenant with Israel, and how do we know that the seven years mentioned in verse 27 are actually seven years? Why can't these "years" be months or decades, or a general figure?

First, we know that the covenant *will be made* with Israel because Gabriel began his discourse by stating to Daniel that the 70 weeks concerned *his* (Daniel's) people and *his* holy city (Jerusalem). We can see this in verse 24. We do not have to guess. So, if Gabriel is telling

Daniel what will happen to his people (Israel/the Jews) and his holy city (Jerusalem), then it is obvious that the *entire* period of 70 weeks deals with events that will be visited upon Israel, the Jews, and Jerusalem ("Seventy weeks are decreed about your people and your holy city…"). There can be no other interpretation without doing damage to the integrity of the text. The *full* 70 weeks is said to be directed *to* Israel and Jerusalem.

If then we have only seen 69 of those weeks fulfilled, then one week of seven years remains. If all the weeks have somehow been fulfilled, then all of this is in the past. Let's not stop here then. We need to find out the exciting conclusion.

Chapter 4

In Between Races

If you have ever enjoyed any type of race at all, whether it was a bike race, a pinewood derby race, a foot race, or any number of other races, you know that they normally do not run concurrently. What I mean by that is that once a race is over, it takes at least a few minutes to check the track, get everyone lined up for the next race and start if off.

Most races are timed, especially if the race is part of an Olympic event. It is important that they not only know who the winner is, but whether or not the winner's time is the best ever to date. If so, they then become the new world record holder for that event.

Jesse Owens and the Olympics

Most of us know of Jesse Owens, but for those who do not, he was an African American gentleman who was a tremendous athlete. In the 1936 Olympics, he was one such individual who represented the United States in a number of events.

That year the Olympics took place in Germany, the heart of Hitler territory. Hitler was intending to prove to the world that the Aryan race of Germany was by far superior to the rest of the world's cultures and population.

Owens won four gold events in four separate events, to Hitler's chagrin. He proved of course that superiority has nothing to do with ethnicity. But the other important point as far as it relates to this subject, is that Owens did not compete in those four events consecutively without any type of a break at all. No one does that.

If we then adopt this outlook regarding these weeks, we will see something similar at work. Once the 69th week had finished, Gabriel states that three things *must* occur and it is obvious from verse 27 that they must occur *before* the 70th and final week *starts*. It is at the beginning of the verse 27 we read the words "*And he shall make a strong covenant with many for one week...*" This then, would be the final week of God's prophetic timetable, which has either already taken place, or is yet future. Verse 27 specifically mentions "one week." If we are going to be consistent here, we must treat this week as we have treated the other weeks, meaning this week equals *seven years*. Some though, prefer to view the first set of weeks as years, equaling 483 years. However, when they arrive at the final week, it all of a sudden represents decades or centuries. If it represents a week of sevens (years) for the first 69 weeks, then the final *week* must also represent years and in this case, seven years. For folks who do this, there is absolutely no logic involved in it. It is obvious that they have chosen to do so for reasons which are purely subjective.

There were two major events (plus an overall world climate), which were slated to happen *after* the 69th week *concludes,* but *before* the 70th week *begins*: 1) Messiah will be killed, 2) Jerusalem will be destroyed, and 3) There will be war to the end, along with desolations.

Give Us a Break
It is obvious that there is a *break* between the 69th and 70th weeks, due to the fact that the 70th week does *not* begin until *after* the events described by Gabriel. The only way to understand these verses in any other light is to apply an allegorical interpretation to the passage, in which case close enough, but not exact is fine for the interpretation. However, even if we stretch things to that extent by claiming that Christ's death caused the sacrifices to cease (which they did *not* by the way), then the "halfway" point that Gabriel mentions is said to be the 70 A.D. destruction of Jerusalem, from the Covenant or Replacement Theologian's position. This is really overshooting the mark though because this one "week" has become roughly 40 years. That is ridiculous. If we understand the passage to be referring to this, then it becomes clear that this event occurs way after what they consider to be the 70th week.

It seems much more logical to understand the two "princes" as two completely *different* people; with the first Prince referencing Christ and the second referencing someone else entirely. Whoever the "he" is referenced here, will make a strong covenant with many for *ONE WEEK*. As mentioned, consistency demands that we interpret *this* week just like the other weeks. So this *remaining* week represents 7 *years* as well.

If you agree with me that the "weeks" totaling 69 weeks or 483 years *ended* with verse 25, and the final 7 years ran immediately *after* the 69 weeks, it would have ended 7 years after Christ's resurrection. What was happening *then* in church history? The Church was building up at that point, and was just beginning to reach out to the Gentiles. In fact, in 38 A.D., Peter was baptizing the *first* Gentile convert.

From 48 to 49 A.D., we read about Paul's first Missionary Journey. If we move three and a half years after Peter's baptism of the first Gentile convert, we are between Stephen's stoning and Paul's conversion. But there is nothing that stands out in 40 A.D., which would have been 7 years after Jesus' crucifixion. Even if we go back to 39 A.D. still *nothing* remarkable stands out on the timeline.

So the point to remember is *not* that time has continued to be *marked* by God, but that Christ's rejection after His successful Triumphal Entry into Jerusalem has effectively *stopped* the prophetic clock. It will remain stopped *until* the 70th week *begins*.

This is very much like the time between the races. Time outside the race track marches onward of course, but the clock that times each race is shut off because it is not needed at that point. It will begin tracking time again when the next race begins, not one second before.

This is what God seems to have done and we know this because of what occurs *between* verses 26 and 27; the events that we have already discussed. These three events (two major events and the world climate) need to happen and we know that the crucifixion occurred and the destruction of Jerusalem happened as well.

Gabriel also stated that there would be war to the end and desolations would occur. This has been the case since Christ's crucifixion. There has *never* been a time of peace in Israel since then. In fact, there was a great dispersion created by God in which all of the Jews were sent or taken out of their land and wound up in places all over the world. This was part of God's plan.

When Israel became a nation again in 1948, while they were accepted *as* a nation by the United Nations, they have *still* not had peace and they do not have peace today either. In fact, Gabriel was clear that the wars and desolations would occur until the end; the end of what? They will occur until the end of the age, which coincides with the end of the Tribulation, when Christ returns physically.

We know from verse 27 that the very last week of Daniel's prophecy as told by Gabriel does NOT begin until "he" makes a covenant with the many. We also know that we do not have an official start date for the 70th week. While the entire 79 week scenario *began* with Artaxerxes' decree to rebuild Jerusalem in 445 B.C. and ran concurrently until Jesus presented Himself as King to the people of Jerusalem, we have *no such* starting point with the final week of God's prophetic timetable, the 70th week. If there was no break at all between the 69th and 70th week, there would be no problem. In such a case, everything would have run concurrently, and it would all be in our past.

However, since Gabriel points conclusively to three separate events that he states occur *after* the 69th week, and *then* the 70th week begins, there is obviously a break or gap in time, which prevents us from knowing exactly *when* the 70th week begins. The Lord does not leave us without clues though. We know that 70th week will begin *when* the covenant is signed with Israel that is supposed to last seven years. This is the official starting point of the last seven years, known as the Great Tribulation.

The Landscape of Church History
Scanning the horizon of history, I am not aware of any covenant that has been made with Israel, since Christ's crucifixion that lasted seven years. While Christ gave a new commandment and instituted a sup-

per in His remembrance, which celebrated the New Covenant, this He did during the 69th week, so that does not count!

In summary so far, we *know* beyond doubt that the starting point Gabriel is referring to is 445 B.C. (Nehemiah 2:1-8). Even though there were previous decrees to rebuild Jerusalem, the only one that seems to matter is the one Artaxerxes issued, because it was with *that* decree that the rebuilding actually began.

We further know that this entire period of 70 weeks is to be fulfilled with Daniel's people and Daniel's holy city. So we understand Gabriel to be saying that these 70 weeks deal with Israel and Jerusalem. Of this, there is no doubt.

We also know that the first two sets of *weeks* run concurrently from 445 B.C. without any break at all. Gabriel divides these weeks of time to let Daniel know what was going to be happening during those periods, but they are not broken up with a pause in between them.

Beyond this, we know that the 69th week concludes in verse twenty-five of chapter nine. Verse twenty-six describes the three events which will occur *after* the end of the 69th week, but *before* the beginning of the 70th week.

Since we do not have the starting date of the 70th week, we have to go by the main clue that Gabriel provides and that is the covenant. This covenant is to be signed with the leaders of Israel (the many), for a period of seven years. This length of time provides us with the knowledge that this is the *final* or the *70th* week of God's prophetic timetable.

In searching history from the time of Jesus' crucifixion, we do *not* see anywhere a period of seven years in which a covenant was signed with the leaders of Israel. Because this has *not* occurred, then we may safely conclude that it is *yet* to occur.

No Reason to Allegorize

There is absolutely *no* reason to spiritualize or allegorize any part of this text. As can be clearly seen, the text speaks for itself, *if allowed* to do so. Those who allegorize the text to make it fit into some type of preconceived notion of what they *think* will take place are not only severely damaging the text, but if they are wrong, they are guilty of *changing* God's Words to mean something other than what they actually mean. Venturing out into this area is like walking a tightrope high above the ground, with no safety net. Great care must be exercised during the interpretive process.

The 69th week has *ended*; this we know for certain because Gabriel states that the 7 and 62 weeks will bring us up to the time of Messiah. It was *after* this the Messiah was killed (cut off), and roughly 40 years later, Jerusalem was destroyed. There have been wars, and desolations which continue through today, and will last to the end of the age. We are at a point in prophetic church history when the 70th week could literally begin at any time. The only thing that needs to occur is what is slated to be the event which takes place at the very beginning, which is the signing of a *covenant*.

One other important point is that while Jerusalem has obviously been destroyed in other ages prior to A.D. 70, *since* A.D. 70 she has been completely destroyed and literally trod *underfoot by Gentiles*. Even though Israel again became a nation in 1948, establishing a position for herself in the Promised Land and Jerusalem, she has only had control of Old Jerusalem *on paper*. In practice, the Temple Mount area and much of Old Jerusalem has continued to be controlled by Muslims who are *Gentiles*, not Jews. This has been the case since 70 A.D. and there seems to be no sign of any change in that situation in spite of the continual rhetoric spoken by politicians.

It was not until 1948 when Israel again took up residence in Palestine that restoration in Jerusalem and other areas of Israel began to take place. However, as noted, the problems which existed for Israel shortly after Christ's death, culminating in Jerusalem's destruction in 70 A.D., continue to be with them. They are a people without peace, in a land where their enemies surround them and will not be satisfied until every Jew is dead or pushed out of the Middle East, or both.

Chapter 5

Last Play of the Game

T he 70th week is either the last play of the game on humanity's part represented by Antichrist's rise to power (the start of the Great Tribulation), or something that has occurred in the past. If the former, it has not happened yet. If the latter, there is nothing to be concerned about, at least not for Christians, but for those who do *not* know Christ. Since God has provided this information, do you not want to know what He is referring to?

He did not provide us with His information so that we could ignore it, or allegorize its truth away. He provided the information so that we could *benefit* from it. Understanding these four verses in the ninth chapter of Daniel is obviously extremely important. It is here that God has taken the time to give us the details of His prophetic timetable! How dare we ignore it, or allegorize it so that it means something else entirely! We have an obligation to know God's mind on this and because He provided the information, we can assume that it *is* discernable. Those who allegorize reap the consequences of playing with God's Word as if it is putty.

It's In the Future
If you consider the fact that Daniel seemed to have *no* difficulty comprehending Gabriel's message and everything that Gabriel told Daniel was yet *ahead* of him, it becomes a question of why is it so difficult for us to understand it. Why are there so many alternate opinions regarding what Gabriel *meant* when he relayed the information?

Since it seems clear enough that the 70th week comes *after* the three events or situations described in verse 26, then it is logical to assume that the 70th week has not occurred yet. If this is true, then a break in the prophetic timetable *must have* begun just prior to Christ's crucifixion. If that occurred, then it is also logical to assume that we are still in that break, which many term a *gap between the 69th and 70th weeks*.

Because the 70th week occurs *after* the events listed in verse 26, it must come later, after these events have all taken place (or in the case of wars and desolations to the end, those *began* in earnest after the 69th week). The 70th week must by its nature (and because of its location in the chronological order) start with something that essentially becomes the *final* seven years of human history.

The end of these seven years comes with Christ's physical return, and the first thing He does is to take out the Antichrist with the breath of

His (Christ's) mouth. He then sets up His kingdom, from which He will reign over the entire world for 1,000 years, from David's throne; the Millennial Kingdom.

It Begins with a Covenant

The 70th week begins with a covenant that a prince makes with "the many." We have discussed this covenant previously, but more needs to be said about it. Beyond this, we need to break this entire verse down in order to know its intrinsic meaning.

The verse reads *"And he shall make a strong covenant with many for one week, and for half of the week he shall put an end to sacrifice and offering. And on the wing of abominations shall come one who makes desolate, until the decreed end is poured out on the desolator,"* (Daniel 9:27).

The word "covenant" has different interpretations and some have taken it to mean that the Hebrew word used here – *Berith* – can only be in reference to a covenant made by God. However, not all agree with that interpretation. Alva McClain states *"the same Hebrew term is used of the treaty made between Ahab and Benhadad (1 Kings 20:34), of the treaty between Ephraim and Assyria (Hos. 12:1), and also of the treaty between Antiochus and Ptolemy Philometer (Dan. 11:22). The same Hebrew word is translated fifteen times in the Old Testament by our English word 'league.'"*[6]

The main sticking point aside from the meaning of the word "covenant" has to do with *who* the individual is referring to in the text. Walvoord makes sense of the potential confusion by stating *"The determination of the antecedent of he in verse 27 is the key to the interpretation of the passage. If the normal rule be followed that the antecedent is the nearest preceding possibility, it would go back to the prince that shall come of verse 26. This is the normal premillennial in-*

---

[6] Alva J. McClain *Daniel's Prophecy of the 70 Weeks* (Winona Lake: BMH Books 1969), 58

terpretation which postulates that the reference is to a future prince who may be identified with the Antichrist who will appear at the end of the interadvent age just before the second coming of Christ. This interpretation is also followed by amillenarians such as Keil and Leupold, as well as by Zöckler."[7]

Antiochus?

Some commentators favor people like Antiochus Epiphanes from the second century B.C. as the person being referred to here, while still other theologians believe the "he" in verse 27 refers to Christ Himself. In order for this "he" to be pointing to Epiphanes, the covenant mentioned here of necessity must be interpreted to be a covenant between the Jews of the aristocracy and Romans of that time period.

In order to maintain the belief that the "he" is Christ, it must be dogmatically maintained that the passage in question concerns Christ *only*, but to assert or assume that means coming to the text with that presupposition already in place. It needs to be *proven* that this is the case. It cannot merely be *assumed* that this is what the text is stating.

To dogmatically assert that the "he" in the text must in both places refer to Christ is the equivalent of stating that there is no possibility that anyone *other* than Christ would be able to make a covenant of any type with Israel from Daniel's time onward.

Beyond this, we must look down through the annals of history past to see if we can find a seven year period of time in which Israel entered into a covenant. Unfortunately for those who take the position that the "he" refers to Christ, there is no clearly distinct seven-year period of time that can be unmistakably discerned.

As Walvoord states, the reality is that *"the question facing every expositor is what interpretation gives the most natural and intelligent ex-*

---

[7] John F. Walvoord *Daniel the Key to Prophetic Revelation* (Chicago: Moody Press 1971), 233

position of the text."[8] This of course is *the* question that must be asked when interpreting *any* portion of God's Word.

Moreover, Walvoord points out that *"If it is not necessary to consider this literal prophecy, and the time units are not literal, a variety of interpretation immediately becomes possible. If the expositor desires to follow the text meticulously, however, there is really no alternative but to declare the entire seventieth seven figure, for there has been no seven-year period fulfilling the events of prophecy, however labored the interpretation."*[9]

No, Not Antiochus
Walvoord and others come to the conclusion that Antiochus does not satisfy the literal demands of the passage. Christ Himself does not satisfy the demands of the text here either since we can find no period in history where He entered into a discernable seven-year period of agreement with Israel. Since Gabriel is giving the details of the prophecy in such a specific way that tell Daniel those details would be recognizable, then to interpret the text allegorically does injustice to it.

Fortunately, we have other portions of Scripture which shed light on this passage in Daniel. By far the most important section is what is found in our Lord's Olivet Discourse, as found in Matthew 24:15-26. It is here that we gain more insight into this last week of human history. There are a number of things that Jesus mentions which are striking in their similarity to the prophecy related in Daniel 9.

If we consider the text in verse 27 of Daniel, we are told that an individual will make a "strong covenant with many for one week." To be consistent, we must take the word *week* here to mean seven years. While the covenant is said to be *strong,* it appears not to be impregn-

---
[8] John F. Walvoord *Daniel the Key to Prophetic Revelation* (Chicago: Moody Press 1971), 234
[9] Ibid, 234

able. Halfway through the week, this same covenant is broken by the same individual who instituted it.

Abomination Redo

In the Matthew 24 passage, Christ discusses the desolation that was caused by Antiochus Epiphanes by referring to Daniel. During the time of Christ, it was common knowledge regarding this desolation that Jesus referred to, as having taken place in 168 B.C., when Epiphanes waltzed into the Temple, slaughtered a pig on the altar, sprinkled the blood around and even set up a statue of Zeus there as well. Some historians note that he put a mask of his face over Zeus' face. In essence, he was claiming to be God and was demanding the Jews worship him as such (since it was their Temple). This event became known as the abomination that desolates. No orthodox Jew worth his knowledge of history and the Torah would not have been aware of this tragic event during the time of Christ.

In reference to this, Christ is basically asserting that the event *will* occur again. He was using the Antiochus Epiphanes event as a point of allusion. He states "*So when you see the abomination of desolation spoken of by the prophet Daniel, standing in the holy place (let the reader understand)*" (Matthew 24:15a). It cannot be denied that Christ is referring to something that is yet future (from His perspective) when He uses the phrase "when you see…" It had not occurred yet, but *would*.

It is because of this that many tend to think of the destruction of Jerusalem and the Temple in A.D. 70 by the Romans as the fulfillment of this event. There are at least a couple of problems with this view. First, in spite of beliefs to the contrary, the sacrifices were not stopped by Christ Himself, some forty years after His own crucifixion. It was the Romans who caused the sacrifices to cease because of their destruction of Jerusalem and the Temple. But the text in Daniel says that "he" who inaugurates the covenant will break the covenant by causing the sacrifices to stop. Unless we view the Roman armies as the "he" in the Daniel passage, this view falls apart.

The other problem is that there was no discernable abomination of desolation occurring during the Roman destruction of Jerusalem and the Temple, as Christ referenced. There would have been no reason for Christ to tell everyone about the abomination of desolation, connecting it with the Epiphanes event, unless it was in fact, going to occur *again* at some point in Christ's future. This is a very clear cut and undeniable event that Jesus speaks of, and it is then obvious that He meant an event which would be *noticed*.

Keeping It Literal
To maintain a literal understanding of the text, we must understand Gabriel to be referring to an event that was *way* into the future. Someone would eventually arrive on the scene, and would come to the leaders of Israel, and enter into a seven-year covenant with them. The covenant would be said to last for seven years. However, after three and a half years, this *same* individual would break the covenant and would do so by committing a similar act of desolation as the one Antiochus Epiphanes had committed a few centuries before Christ.

As Christ relates this desolation to His listeners, He is stating that this type of event would occur at the midway point of the seven-year period and this incident would then mark the midpoint of the *"great tribulation, such as has not been from the beginning of the world until now, no, and never will be,"* (Matthew 24:21). It is difficult to entertain the idea that Jesus was exaggerating here, by making an overstatement regarding the type of tribulation this world would undergo.

Jesus obviously understood that the entire world would suffer at the hands of this one individual and the amount and character of the tribulation foisted upon the world by that person would be such that the world have never seen and would never again see. These are very strong words and undeniable in their conclusion.

Certainly the world has suffered tribulations in the past. There have been two world wars and it appears that we are on the brink of a third, with tensions rising and falling throughout the world on a near-daily basis. Yet, even with these wars, we apparently have not witnessed the type of tribulation that Jesus is referring to here. That is still to come and the horror that will be visited upon this earth during that time is literally unimaginable.

The most interesting reference point in Daniel 9:27 is the very last phrase where Gabriel says that the one who puts the covenant into effect with Israel, and breaks it three and a half years later, is referred to as the *desolator*; *"until the decreed end is poured out on the desolator."* This desolator obviously cannot be referring to Jesus. He is *not* the desolator. The desolator is the one who made a promise with Israel, only to shatter this same covenant by setting himself up as God in the Temple itself, to the shock of the Jewish world.

The sense here is that the abominations of this individual will ultimately turn God's Temple into a house of idol worship. The act of this person setting himself up as God in the Temple, spreads through the entire temple as a cancer, leaving no part of the Temple clean and untouched by its vile presence.

We need only refer to Daniel 12 to determine that this same abomination occurs 1290 days (forty-three months) prior to the return of Christ. If we go from the midway point of the Great Tribulation, 1290 after that, we arrive just inside the Millennial Kingdom.

"And from the time that the regular burnt offering is taken away and the abomination that makes desolate is set up, there shall be 1,290 days," (Daniel 12:11).

We can see in the above passage that the same abomination is referenced and from that point forward, there are 1290 days until the Lord returns. This is obviously referring to the Second Coming and not the Rapture of the Church, since of the Rapture, Christ said no one would know the day nor the hour (Matthew 24:36). The Rapture is also *not* the Second Coming, because during the Rapture, Christ does *not* return to earth. He steps from the throne, out of the third heaven and meets His Bride as His Bride is brought up to Him. He is not coming to earth, He is not returning to earth and because of that, the Rapture is not the Second Coming. The First Advent occurred roughly a little over 2,000 years ago and the Second Coming takes place when He physically returns to earth at the end of the age. The Rapture is *not* the Second Coming.

To Sum It Up

The 70th week holds a mystery, but it is not indiscernible. Gabriel tells Daniel exactly what is going to occur. When we compare the ninth chapter of Daniel with other portions of Daniel and elsewhere in God's Word, we gain greater understanding of just what Gabriel is referring to as he explains the prophecy.

That the 70th week comes *after* the events described in verse 26 is clear. What should also be clear by now is the fact that the events described in verse 26 were not given a specific period of time by Gabriel. They unfolded as was planned, but unlike the first two periods of time – the 7 weeks and 62 weeks – the events in verse 26 had no such time period attached to them. The period of time was essentially left open-ended by Gabriel. It was something that Daniel was not given permission to know by God. God knows of course, but He felt no compunction to share it with either Daniel or us. This clearly denotes that God has put a break in the 70 weeks prophecy. We know this because the actual 70th week does not begin until verse 27 and while we do not know the exact time it will begin, we know the event that will *begin* it; the covenant agreement that takes place with Israel and one individual.

We have shown that the individual in question cannot be Jesus, nor can it be the Roman armies who destroyed Jerusalem and the Temple in A.D. 70.

We have shown that in all likelihood, the person being referred to is the Antichrist. It is he who enters into a strong covenant which is stated to be seven years; the final seven years of Gentile human history of dominance of Israel. It is this same individual who breaks the covenant at the midway point, or three and a half years later. He breaks it by doing something very similar to what Antiochus Epiphanes did in 168 B.C. The Antichrist will set *himself* up as God in the midst of the future Temple, with the resultant defilement causing the sacrifices to cease.

We have also learned that Christ has stated that from that midway point until He returns, the terrible times that will exist on this earth will exist because of the Antichrist and the fact that God is pouring out His own wrath *through* the Antichrist.

Chapter 6

Seeing Things Clearly

The 70th week – if we understand Gabriel correctly – is the last week of Gentile dominance of Israel and Jerusalem; *ever*. It is the last portion of Gentile kingdoms that Daniel learned about and shared with us in Daniel 2 and 7. It represents the second to last stand of humanity against the God of the universe (the very last one occurs toward the end of the Millennium, when Satan is released from his imprisonment in the pit). That is also no contest, because the Antichrist is quickly dispatched by Christ upon His return.

If our understanding of Daniel's 70 weeks is correct, then what remains for planet earth's destiny is *one final week*; the 70th week, otherwise known as the last seven years. After that, it becomes Christ's time to reign physically on earth for a period of 1,000 years. After that, the Great White Throne Judgment, then creation of new heavens and earth and *then* the beginning of the future Eternal Order.

Do Christians have anything to fear? No, simply because it is this author's belief that the Rapture will occur prior to the Great Tribulation spoken about by our Lord. However, *if* the Rapture does *not* occur and the Church is forced to live through the Tribulation, then God will simply *provide*. Those who have faith in God's ability to preserve (even in death) will be preserved.

Living through this horrific period of human history will certainly separate the "sheep from the goats" as it were (though this actual judgment will take place after the Tribulation and prior to the Millennial reign of Christ). However, the Rapture will do the job much better in separating the Church from the upcoming wrath of God. In either case, the truth of the matter is that God and God *alone* will be glorified *through* and *because* of the events that will be visited upon this world. All will eventually bow the knee, either willingly or not, but all *will* bow the knee in recognition of God's absolute supremacy and sovereignty in and over all things.

If Future, When?
When will all this happen? It is simply not known. In fact, those dates and times are known *only* by the Father. For those who keep attempting to discern and set dates, they need to stop their shenanigans because they speak with their own authority which amounts to nothing.

Regardless of the End Times and its reality, we need to live every day as if it is our last on this planet anyway. We do not know when we will breathe our final breath. Because of that, we do not know when the Lord has predetermined in eternity past to take us home to be with Him. We are left here on earth after we become Christians to live for *His* glory. That includes evangelizing as well as many other things that glorify Him.

This world could continue for another 100 or 1,000 years or longer from this point; only the Lord knows. It could also come to an end within the next ten or twelve, or sooner. Again, only the Lord knows when the things *He* has determined will come to pass.

Why Study Prophecy?
In the meantime, what is the point of studying prophecy at all then? There are many good reasons, but three stand out in this author's mind as being the most important:

1. **Knowledge:** Studying prophecy allows the student to gain much more of an overall comprehension of His Word as it incorporates so much more of the entirety of the Bible. This brings Him glory.
2. **Maturity:** Learning more of His Word glorifies God and causes the child of God to grow in grace, strength and knowledge of Him. This also glorifies Him.
3. **Evangelizing:** The child of God is much more equipped to evangelize the world. As we study God's Word, we gain a greater awareness of His timetable and the fact that our lives here are truly very short. The fact that eternity is really only a breath away becomes stamped on our hearts and that creates a desire to witness to a lost and dying world. This points to the Cross of Christ, highlighting His love and forgiveness, both of which glorify Him.

The purpose of studying prophecy is not to become content to simply *know* what His Word says about future events. The purpose of studying prophecy is to become more knowledgeable about His Word in order to be more of an effective witness *for* Him and in order that our relationship *with* Him will grow toward completion. It is the job of every Christian to know what the Bible says about all things, not just prophecy. However, prophecy takes up roughly one-third of the Bible's contents which indicates its importance.

Christians are not left here on this earth after receiving salvation in order to simply enjoy what this life has to offer. Certainly one of our callings is to become a visible testimony of Christ's love and coming judgment to a world that is currently without His love, and facing only His judgment.

Our *highest* calling is to glorify Him in all things; what we *say*, what we *do*, and what we *think*. There is no higher calling for any of God's children; those who have received salvation because of their faith in Christ's redemptive work on Calvary's cross.

This redemption we call salvation must be shared with everyone we can share it with and it is not merely shared with our *mouth*. It is shared in how we *live*, how we *think* and how we *act*. Anyone can talk, but it takes a true Christian empowered by the indwelling Spirit to live out that life of Christ in a world that is in complete rebellion to Him.

Studying Prophecy
Learning and understanding prophecy is a wonderful pursuit; however it does *not* take the place of building up our relationship with Him and evangelizing the lost. It is very easy for Christians to get involved in arguments over this prophecy or that one, which does nothing but wind up serving the enemy. Needless to say, the Lord is *not* pleased because He is *not* glorified in that. I am not referring to defending the faith, which all Christians *must* do. I am referring to

senseless arguments that simply denigrate into name-calling and anger.

We can disagree with one another and still love one another. In fact, that is what we are *called* to do. We are not to allow prophecy to take us off the path of evangelization, and into the area of endless disagreements. If and when we do, we cease to glorify Him.

Paul said it best when he said *"For we do not wrestle against flesh and blood, but against the rulers, against the authorities, against the cosmic powers over this present darkness, against the spiritual forces of evil in the heavenly places,"* (Ephesians 6:12).

Our struggle is *not* with other human beings, though it may feel like that at times. Our struggle is with the powers in heavenly realms. These powers are strong, brilliant, ruthless and deceptive. While they obviously *motivate* human beings to do one thing or another, the struggle is ultimately with *them,* not other people. Our responsibility is to lean heavily upon Christ for the victory that He will provide.

It is for this reason that Paul continued, alerting us to the fact that without God's armor, we are helpless. Once the armor is firmly in place, we *"may be able to withstand in the evil day, and having done all, to stand firm,"* (Ephesians 6:13b).

Knowing God's Word is one of the best ways to stand firm against the enemy. It is what Christ did during His time of testing in the wilderness (and throughout His entire earthly life). For every temptation that Satan through at Him, Christ responded with God's Word and the natural authority that came from it. Satan had no choice but to leave in defeat until he could create other future opportunities.

In fact, we can be assured that in however many ways and times God the Son, Jesus was tempted by Satan, He always responded with the authority found only in God's Word. Satan has no ability to stand against it because in him is no truth at all.

Ramping Up the Evil

As Satan and his cohorts continue to ramp up the amount of evil they cause to be visited upon the people and this planet, a greater attack on the truth of the gospel and His Word in general can be expected. In fact, it is happening now.

Prophetic aspects of Scripture are either directly or indirectly related to the truth of salvation. It makes a good deal of sense then, that Satan *will* do whatever it takes to water down anything from Scripture that may be related to events connected to the End Times. He does not want us going there. He does not want us to be "bothered" by it. He wants to get our minds off of it, hence the reason for all the error that exists today.

With the amount of vitriol that is consistently spewed in reference to anything that even smacks of a literal interpretation of God's Word, it is clear that the enemy has been busy behind the scenes with one attack after another. These attacks have become much more prevalent, and even vicious over the past few decades, showing no sign of diminishing.

Satan is busy doing all he can to subvert God's plans. While he is unable to do this in reality, he must settle for confusing the minds of God's people, and putting them at each other's throats. So far, he seems to have been able to accomplish much. Many who are well known within the ranks of Christendom (and some who are well known for their outright blasphemous views of salvation while calling themselves "Christian"), have joined together in standing against those of us who understand Scripture in literal terms. Please remember though, when we speak of *literal* we are not talking about *literalistic*. There is a huge difference.

Understanding God's Word in its most common, ordinary sense is certainly becoming the minority view. However, this constitutes no proof that His Word should *not* be taken in such a manner.

Because of the absolute accuracy of all the prophecies that have been given and fulfilled in a *literal* fashion, there is absolutely no reason to begin viewing prophecy *allegorically*. If we look back through the Bible to see just how many prophecies Jesus Christ has already fulfilled, the question must be asked, "*Did He fulfill them in a literal fashion, or an allegorical fashion?*" We can and must take our cue from that. The prophecies concerning Christ's birth alone, or the prophecies related to His time on the cross; were these so allegorical that it was impossible to discern their true meaning *until* the events actually happened? Of course not! While figures of speech may have been utilized by the prophets who penned those prophecies, it was fairly easy (to those whose eyes are open) to comprehend the meaning of those same prophecies in *literal* terms.

Why then should we take prophecies related to His Second Coming in any other way but literal? There must be consistency to Scripture, which is not left up to chance, and certainly not left up to man's so-called creative thinking.

We know in fact, that even though Christ *did* fulfill many prophecies concerning His birth, His life, His death and His resurrection, there are groups of people today whose goal in life seems to be attempting to prove that He did *not* fulfill them. This author has personally dealt with Talmudic Jews who have gathered themselves together in groups to fight against what they refer to as missionary endeavors to convert Jews to Christianity.

These groups have written what they at least consider to be hard and fast proof that Christ for instance, was *not* born of a virgin, or that He did *not* fulfill Zechariah 9:9, which speaks of His entrance in Jerusalem mounted on a donkey. In fact, some go so far as to claim that

Jesus never existed at all, but was simply a composite character created by twelve Jewish men, all of whom were outcasts from their own culture and society!

God's Word is beneficial in many ways. But first, it must be understood not as we would *like* to understand it, but as God *means* it to be understood.

We believe that the 70 weeks of Daniel while certainly presented *with* symbolic language, must be interpreted literally. We also believe that the entire 70 week period, including the gap between the 69th and 70th weeks, is best comprehended in a literal sense. Doing so eliminates the guesswork. We no longer are at the mercy of history, trying to determine if the "he" in verse 27 is Christ, the Antichrist, or someone else entirely. The facts become *plain*.

If we are correct in our determination, then humanity has one more prophetic week that may soon be on the horizon, if it is not already there. It will be the worst week man has ever seen. Fortunately, it will also usher in the beginning of the absolute greatest and most blessed time this earth will ever experience; the 2nd Coming of Jesus Christ.

Chapter 7

A Race Well Run

The fact that Jesus is Messiah as well as Savior and Lord is undeniable. Many people though who look only to the Old Testament could not care one iota about the New Testament. These individuals have no need for Jesus and certainly do not see Him as the Messiah. Most who reject Him do so out of hatred and vehemence, which is born of their own rebellious blindness. Some prefer to think that Jesus was a great teacher, but not God.

The Christian needs to be aware of these opinions and the arguments that stem from them. Moreover, it is in the study of prophecy that the Christian can come to the point of being able to show that Jesus was (and remains) in fact the Messiah to Israel and Savior to the world, that was put to death.

It Is All By God's Power
It must be stated here that no human being can win over another human being by strong arguments or even unmistakable proof. For instance, if Noah's Ark was actually located and removed from its position on the top of the mountain where it may still be sitting, chances are great that many would reject that evidence. They would see it, but their brains would reject it as simply being *unbelievable*. Because of their propensity to cynicism, they would begin to create numerous reasons why the Ark that they see with their own eyes is not *the* ark that Noah built which was safely carried above the waters that destroyed the rest of the earth.

The heart of the human being is interesting and to say the least, it will do all that it can do to preserve its own errant thinking as a form of protection, in spite of facing proof to the opposite. This is simply a fact of how the fallen nature operates.

If a person who never believed any portion of the Bible because to him it seemed absurd, ultimately came face to face with something like Noah's Ark, that person's entire world which they spent a lifetime crafting, would face extinction in an instant. Far from letting that happen, they would immediately begin to formulate theories as to *why* the Ark for instance, could not be the real Ark. If it turned out that it *was* the actual Ark, then the focus might turn to the fact that it was not a true *global* flood, or there is no way all the animals said to have lived on the Ark actually lived there for that length of time. This person would not be so ready to allow their own world view to die a quick death.

However, if God by His grace, *opened their eyes* to actually see the truth that is represented by something like Noah's Ark, then normally what results from that eye-opening experience is abject humility. From there, God the Holy Spirit leads them through repentance and eventually to salvation should He choose to do so.

We know about the thief on the cross, who at one moment was reviling Christ and the next not only rebuking the *other* thief who continued to curse Christ, but he himself turned to Christ in humility. This was nothing he accomplished on his own. He was *enabled* to do this because the Holy Spirit removed the blinders from his eyes. Once he saw the truth of *who* Christ was (and remains), he could do nothing but humble himself. That is all that was left for him to do. He had no other options. This humility prompted his request that he be remembered by Christ when Christ came into His own kingdom. This change was *drastic* and *quick* and reveals to us the way in which the Holy Spirit works.

It's Not You, But God
It is because of this that we must never think that our words, our effort, or our vehemence changes the heart of anyone, whether we are discussing salvation or prophecy (and certainly salvation is infinitely more important!). God the Holy Spirit opens the eyes of those He will open and it is only when He opens their eyes, are they able to see and adopt the truth that is professed to them.

God has chosen to use His children in the pursuit of salvation. It is we who have received the Great Commission and it is we who are God's mouthpiece here on earth. God can take our words, our actions or our demeanor and use it to bring salvation to another individual. We speak, we live, and we act in such a way that the message of the gospel of Jesus Christ is expressed to others. It is *God* who may choose to use what we say, how we live and how we act to open their eyes to the truth that is only found in Jesus Christ.

It is the same with prophecy and it is the same with knowing how to show that Jesus Christ is the Messiah that Israel rejected. This can be done in Daniel 9, as one example.

We have seen that if we begin with the correct starting point of Gabriel's prophecy related to Daniel, we will arrive at a time when Jesus is literally riding into Jerusalem on the colt of a donkey. He is there presenting Himself as Messiah. The people respond with a Psalm of praise to Him. He was ordered to stop by the Pharisees because they knew *exactly* what was happening. Christ told them that if they stopped, the rocks would cry out.

Every Christian should be able to prove that Jesus is the Messiah, based on the Old Testament. Daniel chapter nine is merely one example of prophecy that Christ fulfilled, but it is an extremely important one.

Those who do not wish to hear it, or are *unable* to hear it, will be able to hear it only if God opens their spiritual eyes. It is not our position to decide ahead of time who we think will or who will not hear the truth and then act based on that. We must tell everyone we meet and our lives must back up our verbal testimony, so that God *can* use it to bring them to Himself, should He choose to do so. That is our job as Christians.

Cast Your Bread Upon the Waters
We are not to prejudge people. We are not to decide who we will and will not share Christ with, as He must be shared continually with everyone we meet. Christ will take what we provide and use it to glorify Himself, by bringing some to salvation and passing over others. That is His decision and His decision only.

The reality for the Christian is that we can never know enough of God's Word. We must spend the remaining portion of our life on this planet studying His Word, and obeying His will for us by His indwelling power, as it is delineated in His Word.

This short study in Daniel 9 is not an end to itself. It is hopefully a door that will open wide for you regarding the prophecies contained within His Word. I believe that prophecy is an extremely important area to study, but not to simply fill up a brain with knowledge. It is not there in order to enter into foolish extended arguments over this or that area pertaining to some portion of Scripture. It is there to see how God worked, is working, and how He *will* work. It is there to provide comfort to those in His family who question the future.

Ultimately though, prophecy is given to us in order that He might be *glorified*. That is God's chief reason for doing *anything* He has ever chosen to do or will do.

There is no higher purpose for any of God's creatures, but to glorify Him. Is it any wonder that throughout the book of Revelation, there are throngs of saints who remove their crowns and toss them at His feet?

These crowns that Christians will wear in the afterlife are crowns that we did not really earn. It was He and by His power who earned them *through* us. What is a crown compared to eternal life with Christ (unless the particular crown *is* eternal life)? There is no comparison. Eternal life with Jesus is worth more than any amount of crowns we could possibly *win* by the things we do in this life.

It is my prayer that as Christians we will come to see that prophecy is important, but endless *arguing* about it is not. What matters most is how we treat one another and how we evangelize a dying world.

May the Lord bless you and keep you and may His face shine upon you. May we spend our remaining time on this earth, endeavoring to do nothing but glorify Him in all that we say, think and do. Amen.

Resources for Your Library:

BOOKS:

- Basis of the Premillennial Faith, The, by Charles C. Ryrie
- Biblical Hermeneutics, by Milton S. Terry
- Daniel, the Key to Prophetic Revelation by John F. Walvoord
- Dictionary of Premillennial Theology, Mal Couch, Editor
- Daniel, by H. A. Ironside
- Daniel: The Kingdom of the Lord, by Charles Lee Feinberg
- Daniel's Prophecy of the 70 Weeks, by Alva J. McClain
- Exploring the Future, by John Phillips
- Footsteps of the Messiah, by Arnold G. Fruchtenbaum
- Future Israel (Why Christian Anti-Judaism Must Be Challenged), by E. Ray Clendenen, Ed.
- God's Plan for Israel, Steven A. Kreloff
- Israel in the Plan of God, by David Baron
- Israelology, by Arnold G. Fruchtenbaum
- Moody Handbook of Theology, The by Paul Enns
- Most High God (Daniel), by Renald E. Showers
- Mountains of Israel, The, by Norma Archbold
- Pre-Wrath Rapture Answered, The, by Lee W. Brainard
- Prophecy 20/20 by Dr. Chuck Missler
- There Really Is a Difference! by Renald Showers
- Things to Come, by J. Dwight Pentecost
- What on Earth is God Doing? By Renald Showers

Order Other Books by Fred DeRuvo

www.createspace.com • www.amazon.com • www.rightly-dividing.com

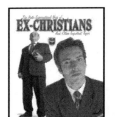

The Anti-Supernatural Bias of Ex-Christians (AVAILABLE)
Look into the testimonies of folks who refer to themselves as Ex-Christians. Are they, or are they kidding themselves? Fred goes back to the Bible to determine the truth of their words. Other topics deal with the Rapture, the Israelites as slaves in Egypt and more. 240 pages, $11.99, 7 x 10 format

When the Rightful Owner Returns
Prophecy has become more of an interest to many Christians lately and with it, varying ideas related to the End Times. Is there any way to know for certain what the Bible actually teaches? Fred believes there is and it starts with a right understanding of the Bible. 235 pages, $10.99, 7 x 10 format

Christianity Practically Speaking
As a Christian, do you ever feel like it's just not working, where the rubber meets the road? Is it your expectations, the Bible's, or a bit of both? Fred seeks to explain Christianity in practical terms that every Christian can appreciate. 235 pages, $10.99, 7 x 10 format

Unlocking Israel's Heart
Romans chapters nine through eleven deal with Israel as it relates to the future. Paul seems clear enough that there is yet a future for Israel, yet not all would agree. Is there a way to be clear about what Paul says? Does the nation he loves have a future? 235 pages, $10.99, 7 x 10 format

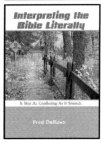

Interpreting the Bible Literally (AVAILABLE)
unfortunately, too many Christians today are not aware that in order to study and interpret Scripture, certain tools (or methods) must be applied. It's like learning a foreign language, complete with idioms and other forms of figurative language. 235 pages, $10.99, 7 x 10 format

Made in the USA
Charleston, SC
19 January 2010